I Live in the Country
& other dirty poems

Also by Arielle Greenberg

Come Along with Me to the Pasture Now

Locally Made Panties

Slice

Home/Birth: A Poemic (co-written with Rachel Zucker)

My Kafka Century

Given

I Live in the Country
& other dirty poems

Arielle Greenberg

Four Way Books
Tribeca

for "the community," as we say in "the lifestyle"

& for Mikey, the animal at the center of the diorama of this particular habitat (which makes me a very lucky girl indeed)

...and I thought well as well him as another and then I asked him with my eyes to ask again yes and then he asked me would I yes to say yes my mountain flower and first I put my arms around him yes and drew him down to me so he could feel my breasts all perfume yes and his heart was going like mad and yes I said yes I will Yes. (Molly Bloom in James Joyce's *Ulysses*)

&

Sexuality is the lyricism of the masses. (Charles Baudelaire)

&

I believe in the radical possibilities of pleasure, babe. (Bikini Kill's "I Like Fucking")

&

...force takes me by the throat into the darksweet corner of my own mind. (Kristin Sanders in *CUNTRY*)

&

Children know something they can't tell; they like Red Riding Hood and the wolf in bed! (Nora in *Nightwood*, Djuna Barnes)

& also reminding myself that

Something always seems to go wrong somewhere between desire and revolution. (Guy Hocquenghem)

Library of Congress Cataloging-in-Publication Data

Names: Greenberg, Arielle, author.
Title: I live in the country & other dirty poems / Arielle Greenberg.
Description: New York : Four Way Books, 2020.
Identifiers: LCCN 2019031753 | ISBN 9781945588433 (trade paperback)
Subjects: LCSH: Women--Sexual behavior--Poetry. | Country life--Poetry. |
Erotic poetry, American.
Classification: LCC PS3607.R447 A6 2020 | DDC 811/.6--dc23
LC record available at https://lccn.loc.gov/2019031753
This book is manufactured in the United States of America and printed on
acid-free paper.

Four Way Books is a not-for-profit literary press. We are grateful for the assistance
we receive from individual donors, public arts agencies, and private foundations.

This publication is made possible with public funds from the
New York State Council on the Arts, a state agency.

We are a proud member of the Community of Literary Magazines and Presses.

Contents

I Am an Animal

First I was an animal.

First I wanted be an animal who survives, who lives, who eats yolk and red fruit, who drinks clear water, who sleeps down in a tight thick curl all winter, who daisy-faces toward the summer sun when it peeks out, who runs, who hungers, who fucks.

First I wanted to fuck, to turn this moment all the way into my flesh like a starred sky and think of nothing else, to explode.

First I wanted to explode and be exploded into, to wet all over, to be filled with creamy life, to be sticky, to be pregnant.

First I wanted to be pregnant, to breed, to extend past the length of my own bruised limb, to sow, to expand everywhere like a broke-up seed, to burst in the dirt of it all.

First I wanted to birth, to moan and quicken with the moon and squat in the dawn and push and scream the names of gods I never cared about before, to pop the blood in my eyes with the effort, to split in half up the ass, to come as close to death as possible, to loll a head out of my vagina and squat there, doubled, mothered, knowing it.

First I wanted to mother, to eat the smell of new skin, to feed this babe

3

from my own calloused and bitten inches, to feed on its love, to never sleep, to sleep like fur, to obsess, to squirt milk when I made myself cum in the dim few hours alone.

First I did not want to cum. I wanted to do nothing but nurse and sleep and not-sleep and prod gently at my other body as if it were a fossil beneath the deflated and heavy fat of my body, and to mother. I wanted to mother that baby right up.

First my baby stood up and stopped nursing and I wept and let my arms hang down and went for a run and my body excavated itself from the extra fat and something sparked in me, a flint that was that other kind of animal sense again, tiger bear firefly wolf bunny buffalo bitch in heat, that was my libido that wanted to fuck, and I set the baby aside in a safe warm nest and went out hunting.

Again and again. A cycle of seasons, of mating and fucking and sleeping dormant and breeding and raising up cubs and sniffing their slipperiest hairs, their powdery drool of wanting.

It comes. It flows. When I am full of a child, and then when my arms are newly full of a new child, we are a bubble on a stream, and I am practically nothing but milk and lowing. Then the child walks and the milk dries and my body thins and all I can think about is skin and tongues and fat and muscle again. And then I want to fuck and I want to cum and I want to be knocked up and I want to only carry this baby so its heartbeat is directly up against my heartbeat and I want to sleep and I want to run in the mud and I want to dance and I want to eat red meat and I want to fuck.

Because first, blessedly, I am an animal.

"Made by Maid" is My Favorite Song by Laura Marling and I Want to Crawl Inside It, and You, Too

gunners in my stomach
the almost-throw-up feeling of sex want

    & the animal in the kitchen wall
        behind the oak secretary
        scratching, having fallen down a tub or tube

                (which maybe I am also falling down??)

& everything opening with the taint & tease
      of spring
      on the wet lips of February on the Maine coast

everything trying to come out

but   *no sir   no sir*
              on my knees sir
(I kind of like saying it)

I will stay here in my deep swallow
I will keep choking   fake choking

I will imagine again & again the first time we meet
      the earth cracking beneath our flat black shoes

the apocalypse changes nothing
it is excruciating & gorgeous
            (all the jeweled food in the mason jars repeating like chant)

keep me like that   for a special occasion

a wound watch skipping in its little jittered second
as a means to a lucid state: *check it*

I'm forgetting to eat, even; it's so unlike me

            all the yous in the universe
            make a hot ravine down the middle of my tongue

A Wild Way

berries cupped

in front of your body

    & berries cupped

    inside your body

    so I am dripping like a garden:

        >> *just fucking fuck me please* <<

a walnut:

    a plum:

a beckoning:

        >> GRAY WOLF <<

               pin me down!!!

no   you say

let's take it
    one step
    on a smooth gray stone
    at a time

                      oh sweet wild plum
                      with your gloves on

& I will keep the berries near my skin
& I will also find another to take me
          a wild way

Friend to the Farmers

come eat by me and be my love:
I made you this, with whole wheat flour

this is what it means that whole wheat flour is whole:
      it has the bran, the germ and the sperm left in it

      so do you, thank god

and me   I am a wholesome girl
friend to the farmers!
      which means I am often dirty
      even filthy
      here in the country
and have to wear my knee-high spaceship-silver shit boots

      (everyone in the country wears knee-high boots in mud season)

I am a natural, free-ranging milk-fed girl
      SO wholesome

though I don't really like to think of my mouth or my cunt
as holes because they have so much happening inside them

but come along with me

we will all the pleasures prove

I Live in the Country

I live in the country.

In the woods.

Take a dirt road to find my little firebox, my tinder.

Something about "bush-hogging."

The pastoral clogs my face and plugs me wholesale.

I do not live in the woods, really.

Joel says, *You don't live in "rural Maine."*

I live in town.

Town is where you see people who are your neighbors and sometimes want to fuck them by the bulk whole wheat pastry flour at the Co-op.

Men think like this all the time, I've been told.

The roving eye. The constant cataloging.

The log, the drift, the wood.

I've got to get some wood going in the morning.

Start the morning with wood.

For a fire.

(Roving is the wool fluff
in clumpy strands spun straight from the wheel.
You can use it in felting:
make something with a needle,
poking it in here and here.)

Chassis

the moon is full tonight, nearly
my gut knows it
no   you misheard me   I said my cunt knows it
no I said my wolfy hair curls from it

but I only saw her from the kitchen window tonight
& didn't even roam   into any forest at all

which is, after all, what I came here to the country to do

*

what good is a community
in the slosh between winter & spring,
when I live inside my head-house with the fire going?

what good's an open marriage
when I'm so goddamned choosy
& don't go outdoors when the moon pulls my name?

*

everyone here has a truck
         has a pick-up

& what I love about men is how they are *men*
the whole goddamned machine of them
     the chassis
     the engine
     the driveshaft
     the flatbed
how they constantly jack off into their own big hands
how they are "hard-wired"—as I have come to believe—
to ignore context & just see the damn trees

*

I do understand them, actually
they make total sense to me
the way you know where to put me even if you're not built like I am

*

trust your "totem animal"
trust the "moon"

*

I have come
which is an act of believing
I have believed this way probably 12,000 times in my life so far

*

& you are hard now
it makes me wired to know so
how you act like your chromosomes
when the silver disc is lodged in my throat
no I said my throat

no I said
just tell me where you want to put me
& what you want to do

The Boy (Inappropriate)

The marriage I am in has just opened, and I am playing with *meeting people on the internet*, which feels like the ridiculous simulation of connection that it is. A boy—a poet; someone's student, though not mine—arranges to pick me up in my small town and we drive over country roads through rain showers and double rainbows, past falling-down farms and doublewides, toward a hotel in an office park in the middle of a field and close to a university.

I feel mostly soft syllables in his direction from my leather passenger bucket seat in his blue VW Passat. Mostly rainy moments I feel. On the drive we talk openly about the problematic lack of discourse around the possibilities of pleasure and joy in heterosexual male desire. We pull organic apricots and goat cheese in olive oil out of his backpack and put them on at a picnic table at a rest area sponsored by the Eagle Scouts. We talk about French translation. He eats quinoa. I eat quinoa. Earlier, before we'd left my town, I'd bought him a beer at the food co-op—which is illegal, because he is not yet of drinking age—but we didn't bring a church key, and despite the fact that he is a college student, he can't find a way to open it without one.

The boy is a farmhand for the summer, manning—boying—the farm stand. He was bearded when I first saw him on webcam, and I instructed him to shave it off, so today at the Eagle Scout park he has no beard. He kicks his Birkenstocks off into the grass in front of the picnic table. (He plays soccer, and wants to do it sometime on his field.) He likes it when I drink water out of my mason jar, when I tell him I canned pears, that I made kale salad for dinner.

The plural noun *exploits*, meaning *daring adventures*, is kin to the term *exploitation*, I remind myself. But I am trying to be with everything as it happens, as a way to "deconstruct the power differential." The double rainbow. The soft syllabics. At a traffic light on a country road, I turn to him and ask how he's feeling. *Intimidated*, he says, *and giddy. Terrified. I'm nice*, I say. *I'm wholesome. I'm friendly.*

This boy is a boy, truly. We both like how it is inappropriate. He thinks the blond clerk at the hotel desk can see it, looks at us funny, which makes us both happy. As does the notion of doing it in public (which we do not do with each other). As does poetry, the kind of poetry uttered like a stuttered double sermon, the kind of poetry partially erased by a philosophical fog, so we check in quickly, before the reading by the famous poets begins. When I stop to pee first I am surprised to find my panties soaked, like they were at twelve around any nice boy I knew.

The boy is a Catholic, with a Catholic mother who thinks he's at a sleepover. A Catholic mother the same age as my own husband. My own husband, who knows I'm here with the boy. Who will shake his hand heartily when we return to my house.

We go, me and the boy, to hear an erasure project, to hear an Italian woman discuss the "modalities of torsion." We are doing something that might get called *deviant*. In fact, we have so far done nothing but eat apricots. I have ruffled his thick hair one time.

In the lecture hall before the reading starts we play Who Would You Do? Because of the boy, I consider the college students texting in the audience, previously off-limits. In all my time spent with college boys as their teacher—nurturing them, really, and egging on all their jack-off poems—I never fucked a one. Never even thought of it. Now I reconsider how it may have landed in all the one-on-one office hour meetings and the slight smiles under thick boy hair as I would say *More poems about your morning wood. Those are good.* But I meant it—those were their most honest poems—and I did not ever want to fuck them, or want them to fuck me.

The boy and I sit next to each other chastely for the reading by the notoriously difficult and important American poet, who sways vigorously at the podium like the old Jew he is, and the boy laughs at all the tricky and correct places, and this is why I decide I will maybe fuck him later. This and because, when I lean in a bit, he smells of his boy-ness.

We are at a poetry conference, me and the boy. His first. My many-th. I am among friends and colleagues. He is among idols. We are possibly deviant, inappropriate. These poets know I am married. The boy looks like a boy. The boy looks like a boy but we have the same CDs jammed between the front seats of our cars, and the boy was listening to Philip Glass when he pulled up to my family home to collect me.

It's a poetry conference about the 1980s. Halfway through the introduction of the first poet, I lean over and whisper to the boy, *It's a conference about a decade from before you were born.* At the end of the last reading, when the important poet reads work from "the end of the decade," the boy leans over and whispers to me, *Still not born yet.* I laugh and feel my panties fill again.

"In the Pines"

In order to have the sex I wanted
I had to leave the city
& go to the country
where the animals are

I took off all my clothes at the trailhead
& walked through the woods
like some video for an Icelandic rock song

I had to be made of the ice breaking up in the creek
I had to be in the pines
I had to go over the falls again

*

      oh my hot & pink little cunt-tree
      with the animals in it
      & birds alighting on all my softer skins
      & snow melting out of my greener eyes
      & sap running sweet to a song
      in the veins of my cunt-tree when the nights snap silver

      but the days are slowly & definitely warming

*

I had to put on my fox-fur ears
I had to put on my snow-white bunny tail
I had to leave the city
& twitch my tongue at the shepherd in his wooden hut
& the milkmaid in her milking house

*

I live here now
        eager to be found

I Lay on the Shore Naked this Morning at Dawn and Thought Again about Submission

On the Pantone scale of pain and pleasure,
find me at willow green, that switchy square   between weeping and
the beautiful, cleanliness and root.

I mean, there is no part of me that wants
to vacuum-seal your cock in black latex like I see on FetLife,
or be choked so hard I vomit peas,
but I do desire—
     I do so desire—
the line you make with your hands when you watch me walk away,
otherwise known as The Hourglass,
     or how you say something thick and approving
     when I tell you later how another man
     dabbed me in the held breath of his lust for a moment—
     but how I gave away to him nothing.

Nothing I contain is flat.
All around my bared and sun-warmed body,
snails are fucking each other,
brown and slick and slow in their sandy little homes.

Baking

You take all the goodliness:

      the flour from the flowering stalk

      the cocoa from the small bean

      the eggs from the laying hens

      the sugar cracked from the hard cane

      the salt and its licking

Put them in my bowl   and muddle

Afterward, I am shining with plant life

skin scratched to newness   flush with animal protein

in my throat   and hair   and os and cheek

and cervix   and eyes

I am tilled and plowed and heated through

and I come out delicious

Three hours later, you muddle again, harder

      That's one of the things I like so much about you

The Pornographic Imagination

It takes three to seven minutes to iron a man's shirt,
which is also the average time

it takes an average man
to reach climax during fornication.

You say it makes you feel like a man to see me bend over
and undo the button at the back of my skirt.

And what does that mean, to *feel like a man*?
Are we talking about hormones?

About constructs? You say
you can while away the time spent in line at Whole Foods

looking at the cute girl in combat boots buying spelt flakes,
and that in three to seven seconds

you can picture what she'd look like
kneeling in front of you sucking you off.

My husband says it's constant, a stream:
I could do her, and I could do her,

whoever happens by. My brother-in-law says
every second he is not thinking about something specific,

he is pulling something out of the mental spank bank.
Every *second.*

This, I guess, is what it is to feel like a man.
A person who transitioned from female to male

said that after the first injection of testosterone,
the next day—the next day!—

it was as though the whole world
had turned into a candy-colored porno film,

fantasy hardcore action with every girl who passed.
Believe me: this is not how *my* mind works,

and I think it's safe to say I think about sex *a lot.*
Maybe more than most women. (I possibly have more testosterone,

which could also explain a few other things about my personality.)
But I don't think like that, not cinematic scenarios called up at will.

How do men *live* in the world?
How do they get any work done?

What vast volume of energy goes into tamping it down,
flicking it purposefully off,

that could be otherwise channeled into peace accords
or electric car engineering? While you sit here trying so hard to focus,

let me take the first sip of your second beer,
the one I teased you into buying.

I have much on my mind that is *not* wall-to-wall. It's been a long day
of global problem-solving with my crystalline estrogen brain,

and maybe your foamy vision is contagious.
I'd like to catch a bit of it, so pass me your flip-topped can.

And a Brief Memo on Impossibility

I am not *trying to ignore rape.*
I am not ignoring rape, specific or writ large.

I am trying   to turn my eye toward joy.
My heart toward bliss.
To turn my fist toward possibility.
Toward your g spot.

I am being a feminist in the misogyny.
I am being a femme in the tidal wave of the gaze.

"The 'non-viable' has its own charge."—Myung Mi Kim

Chat

to keep me writing the essay I need to get in on deadline
I tell you to pat me on the head
tell me how proud you are of me for working

this is sometimes called (derisively) "topping from the bottom"
how an s-type instructs their D-type on how to dominate them

but really it's just standard-issue healthy power exchange
the way you are eager for me
and through your eagerness I hold the power
and I decide when I want you to take it back

this is the power I've always most wanted
the one I hold and then hand over like bear skins

10:38 AM **Eager:** are you working?
11:25 AM **Eager:** sure seems like you're being a good girl
Daddy's very proud
11:28 AM **me:** {serious, scholarly nod}
Eager: good girl
{pat pat}
11:29 AM **me:** ha, I'm just reeling from how it's all so fucked up in this
perfect, crazy way.

11:30 AM **Eager:** I just thought of that too

11:31 AM **me:** I'm writing this piece about Second Wave feminism and escaping from the hetero-axis where women are seen as powerless girls . . . and then I check in and you're patting me on the head and calling me a good girl. WILD.

Eager: and you can own it all

me: well, I don't know. But I am formulating ideas about this kind of negotiated erotic power exchange for a poem.

Eager: perfect!

11:32 AM **me:** yes, but that's the big question for me—how to own my consensual submission within what is still a completely misogynist system. Is it possible to genuinely own (and therefore consensually overturn) that kind of power, the power of surrender? I want to believe it is . . .

Eager: well, it does become challenging when you take power exchange in the context of the whole culture, since there are so many people who don't or won't understand it in an erotic, healthy, sane way

me: the notion of power exchange between a dominant man and a submissive woman seems like maybe a game of pretend within the patriarchy, a game of faking it till we make it to someplace beyond a rape culture. People say you can only give power if you have power to give—like how I am choosing to play-act at being "submissive" when out in the world I am not, just as you are mostly not "dominant" unless we are playing that you are—

31

11:33 AM **Eager:** there are pockets of enlightenment in the kink community where this kind of consensual power exchange feels safe and understood

me: But none of this exists in a vacuum. The good girl story, the submissive woman story comes from somewhere, and the place it comes from is strewn with misogyny.

Eager: stupid men, always ruining everything

me: I think more than "safe" or "understood" I want to find the place where erotic power exchange feels "authentic" and "radical."

11:34 AM **Eager:** gotcha

okay, get back to work

{smack}

me: ooof!

11:35 AM **me:** I'm going to put this whole chat in the poem, I think.

I will take that name they'd call me and bend it backwards
and wear it as a fascinator

I will turn this corner
in my thrift store high heels

I will look at you
I will look at myself with my own gold eyes

and know what I know

all those songs about some girl getting off her knees
I won't be on my knees for you, she sings
But I will
I will be on my knees

I take the money out of my soft verdant wallet
I buy you a boiled wool coat
I buy us a night in a luxe hotel
I buy us a night in an off-the-grid cabin

but the whole time I'm hoping you'll grab me
throw me down
while I tell you that you own me

this kind of power is in the photograph and the throat
the lipstick and the spank
the collar and the slow gait

this kind of power is in the copies of *Playboy* my dad kept
inside the hollow behind a concrete end table
in the formal living room unused except for company
and which I found and looked at and loved

and read choice in the Bunnies' wide-eyed masks
and read their heat as power

I was maybe wrong then
and maybe wrong now
but I want to dwell in the hole where it is possible

Hiding

I admit it: I am hiding from my life in the graveyard of sex, dirty deep pleasure dugouts. Crypts and cozy nooks. Lust of the kind of one-track focus most often associated with zombies, the kind that pushes on the breastplate, goes below and in.

I hide and hide. I hide inside my body, keeping both hands by my solar plexus. I hide in her body, inside the enamel of her teeth and the vortex at the small of her back. I hide in his body, the meaty inches that span his side from back to chest. I hide in a group of bodies, up on a picnic table, down on some sticky plastic inflatable sex furniture, on the newly sheeted mattress at the back of the club. I hide inside the delirium of my physical, inside the launch pad of attraction, the event of sex, the vacuum seal of my orgasm. Its waterfall. Its waterfall.

I smile so wide when I get there.

Beyond this natural history diorama, there is still my life, with the anxiety and the meal plans and the roof shingles scattered in the yard. There is still my little town, with the DUI crashes and the meth lab up the street. There is still my rural county, with the same-named families in the falling-down farmhouses with the broken trucks in the yards and the kids smoking by the library after they've been kicked out and that one house on the corner with the Confederate flag raised behind a tall wooden fence. There is still my state, my nation, my nation-state, my continent, my hemisphere, my planet.

But sometimes I do hide, for three or twenty or eighty-eight minutes, inside the glowy delight of the prospecting that goes on where all the little lights do not shine.

I Have to Leave the Country

In order to have the sex I want
I have to leave the country for the weekend
and go to the city
where we are feral, human

*

standing in the elevator machine in the hotel by the harbor full of gulls
    and ships
my bones and skin just in front of your bones and skin
we are still two human animals, two human animals inside a bright
    metal box
so when you press your hard primate-side inside its soft layers of
    clothing
against my slippery primate-side inside its soft layers of clothing
I immediately back up into you, without thinking, and rub and slide
    along you as we ascend

through the hotel by the harbor full of lights and animals
to pace down the carpeted hallways to our corner room
where we turn off all the electricity
and build a little fire on the nightstand
so I can crouch on all fours
and scream into something dark and furred and out-of-doors

A Mothering Hole

in the new country life
I am mostly in a mothering hole—
I mean a mothering role

it's a wholesome hole

(and how do you think all those babies got in there?
one was by plan
and two were by my see-saw libido
postpartumly whacked back up in my face
until I wore the man down)

(sometimes even a person with babies
forgets how those babies were made)

(even I sometimes forget this, forget that a loving mother
can be someone who wants to be fucked by an almost stranger,
the one having very little to do with the other)
as I was saying, in the new country life

I drive the baby over this rutted dirt road in spring
to a mother-child morning class
at the wood-and-felt school in the woods
with the chickadee dee dees at the feeder and the laying hens

and the one black sheep
with her wild clear eyes
who "may or may not" be pregnant
(you'd think the owners would be able to tell
but who I am to say what a farmer ought to know about her flock?)

it's all very wholesome:
the brown rice and flax seed oil in the wee china bowls
set out on batiked cotton cloths
the plant-dyed yarn we mothers are instructed
to sit and knit into squares to make little balls
we will stuff with carded wool
while the children sweep up the heart pine floors
with enamel dustpans and do the washing-up
of the tiny drinking mugs in the basins full of warm water
and lavender oil and shit bare-assed on the dirt
under the picnic table outside

in her long flowered dress and woolen slippers
the teacher skips about the perimeter of the round braided rug
and I am standing in the way,
thinking about sex with an almost stranger
"won't you skip with us?" she asks me

at circle time, the teacher sits on the floor across from me
and under her long dress I can see the holes
in the crotch of her space-dyed cotton tights

I have a little pussy
she teaches us to sing
her coat is silver-gray

when I lived in the city and thought about moving to the country
I too imagined I might wear a long flowered dress and work boots while
    keeping house
but the little lingerie shop downtown just called
and my black satin garter belt finally came in
and I plan to wear it with white lace stockings with seams up the back
for sex with an almost stranger
after which I may or may not still wear them
while I do the washing-up

Shearling

named for a lionness,
I want to lie down with the lambs

so I cover my mattress with a king-sized sheepskin
top my sheets with a blanket of undyed wool
coat my freshly shaven legs with lanolin cream
and hand you the birch paddle lined on one side with shearling

in this way I am made peaceful

*

the truth is, since starting to have all this new sex
I don't read the Sunday *Times* much anymore
I click off NPR with its many disasters
replace *The New Yorker* on the nightstand with *The Ethical Slut*
turn my mind inward like a rose-colored asshole

I want to live in a warm unlit place
a little shelter made of flesh
like a fucking drop-out (a *fucking* drop-out)
a back-to-the-cunter

*

am I not, as the Buddhists say,
generating compassion in the world by starting with myself,
between my thighs?
or does filling my mouth with cock to quiet and empty my mind
make me an escapist, a runaway?

I know that sex is tied to current events
and I do care about the whole planet
but sometimes I only want to stroke one or two or five members of it
(separately, sometimes together)
as a very concentrated political act of pleasure

*

but this is me thinking again
so here is the soft side, with lamb's fur

now please put me over your knee

It's a Black Box Theater

I perform my gender in the dream of men.

I'm not stupid.

Bread&butter.

So do we all.

The audience is singular, one-eyed and vicious.

I dance anyway, slippery and beyond.

At the Time of the Year when the Veil is Thinnest

the lost & found place   the wooded place the dark moon place
          I go to to be lost & found when you say   sweetly
cocksucker   & I am tuned to the frequency of your   hard-
on   & all else within me   under a black net veil   lost
     found   while I pulse my throat   its red workings to the slick
vegetal heat of you   leaking like I'm leaking   the synchronicity
     jolt   of our matched arousal
  which does it for me every time brother   Daddy   boy   oh boy
the sheltered place   lost   the lean-to place   found the
starred place where   I pull you in   push you back   against your
own oaken trunk   I am the creator-root   molten you are
the root   the first chakra   bursts open like a Japanese
pinball flower   I stuff your cock into my throat my   fifth
chakra to spring the cobalt blue language there   *do you*
like it like this?   *oh you like that don't you*   *you*
love filling my holes   little *wet holes* because my ears are
seashells   & you are in them   & in me   I am as small as
the ocean   massive & indivisible my children are not in here with
me   now my money is not in here with me now my poems are not
in here with me now   mostly   my
ambition not here   my lists of groceries   my   anxiety   lost   &
found   just the backward lick   of my feminist politics   bent & purple
but intact   a taste I have come to know when I am   the queen of wands
& this golden-coin world is one of many gods I can swallow down hard

Divining Rod

It's the balsamic moon, mid-April,
the near-waned phase between Seed and Hare,
insemination season, and the thirteen women
are meeting again in the house perched in the still-bare trees
by the salt marsh to talk about how our joy-sorrows
align with the stars and planets under which we were born.

How do I say to these kind, careful, hurting women
that what I *want* is horsepower,
which here in the country often refers to a small farm
where actual horses drag actual logs in from the woodlot,
but what I mean is *your* horsepower,
you hung like a horse and engaged in the biology of your power?

How to say that when you say *I want to fuck you till you see stars*
and then keep pounding I am engaged in the biology of my power,
and am taking it as the sweetest endearment possible?
That I am taking it, gladly?
How I *like* it? And how you like it when I like it,
and it makes you go harder,
which is how I like it?

How do I tell this story to the woman in the moon circle
whose brother did something to her when she was a little girl
that she did not want him to do
and who has just sat with him while he has told her
that before she was born,
someone did something to him he did not want them to do?
And she held him as he cried, and said that later, maybe,
she will put a gun to his head?

I'm talking about consent.
The difference between a spring divined on one's own land
with a willow switch and an oil pipeline drilled through seized, plowed
earth from here to Alaska.
I'm talking about pleasure versus violence.
And I'm saying I sometimes want it rough.

I'm saying some of us might enjoy being
divined with a willow switch.
Some of us might enjoy being called *Little Girl* while being rammed
with something long and hard.

Women.   Men.   Circles.

Power.   Stars.   Rods.

Horses.   Bullshit.

Animals treated cruelly,

and animals enjoying the work to which we've evolved.

Some of the women in the circle—

the Aries (rams) and Tauruses (bulls)—

are having birthdays,

and some of them are eating chocolate cake,

and some of them are crying,

and one of them has a husband who brought her to a spring he found in

the woodlot on their farm

for her birthday, and as another gift bought her soft moosehide shoes.

I look up every night for the stars

here where I have moved by the mountains by the sea,

and I see them. I see stars.

I'm fertile again this resting moon, and restless,
and engaged in the work of dowsing my body
for all its hidden gems and gravesites,
its alchemy, its thick oil and clean water.

Girl on Girl

You have a sheaf of shiny tamarind-orange hair
and you say *Holy smokes!* in gosh-mouthed delight
when cinched into the black satin 24-inch-waisted corset-dress
that shows up how white your Irish skin

and you know how to make yourself gush onto the hotel towel

and you came down from the mountain where you built your house and
    birthed your babies

and made me laugh so hard at dinner my jaw hurt
and later, let me put the tip of my tongue
on all your folded peach places.

Later still, you lay with your daisy face
four inches away from my face
while my boyfriend plowed me from behind,
and when I called out, uncontrollably, *Daddy*
I saw you open your own mouth in stunned, shared pleasure,
which became what I remember, even more than the plowing.

Later still, we put ourselves in pigtails and cheer skirts
and knee highs and held hands
and walked through the buffet-line gauntlet in the restaurant

shuddering giddily with the silliness
of trying to brace ourselves in the undertow of the gaze.
Your husband told us how two men passed,
turned back, and collapsed against each other in our wake.

So then we skipped.

And the next day, I taught you how to knit.

And you told me about your oldest, anxious boy.

And we scissored our legs under soft sheets
in a heap of true-cliché and matched up our sticky.
It was so like a porno, I suppose,
but we were a four-legged, two-mouthed creature,
bigger and more seashelled than anything imaginable.

Hand-Fasted

Monogamy was invented for farmers:
       tied to your land, tied to your lover,
       wedded, yoked, reliable as an ox come spring.

As animals, we learned the art of staying put.
       Under a rock. Under a stone.

My particular tribe is known for spangling our eyes and wandering,
in units of forty, through floods and parted seas,
melting our bangles for the dance party,
but trying always to find (and fight) a home promised like a star.

      And the shepherd-king David and his soul-mate Jonathan hid
          by the south side of the stone
      and took off Jonathan's robe and sword
          and they wept and kissed
      and were warm in the glow of their buggery.

It was different, no, when we lived in a pack?
And we fuck-all'ed the red tent and our many husbands
and sisters and also-gods?

And before we came together as tribes, weren't we more like
canines, hunters on our raw legs, a moving ring
who made fires at our centers?

Now that we have gathered,
how do I show you I love you near my hearth?
That I love you returning to my children?
That I love to put the pots to boil for you,
and press my nose to your shoulder?
And that, at this moment, I see it lasting quite a while?
What if there is no paper, no court, that will marry us?

Not a farmer, not a nomad.
Not a white buffalo, not a gazelle.

I will love you and lay you a year and a day,
and thee mine, and then we shall see, won't we,
and think on it again,
after the wheel of the seasons has turned over all its plain skin.

Gee

Typically, my clit's a dull joint:
a pretty lounge with piped-in Muzak.
I'd rather it was just skipped.

> Once a moon, tho, right as my blood
> is done and oxi-brown,
> it gets all sudsy and carbonated in there,
> the head of one's fave cold beverage.
> For those brief hours, I want it
> endlessly tweaked and torqued,
> lashed into the seam of my jeans
> till I rocket. Even so,
> it's an itch, not the bomb of blissed-
> out butterflies I've heard described.

Nope, I'm a g-spot girl all the way,
always have been, since infancy (so the story goes):
rocking my crib to glaze-eyed seizure.
I don't know how I knew to do it.

My tulip's in the bulb, deep-seeded,
a tight purple clot only reached

by hammer, nailed (harder please),
and which I can only reach by clamping down
against some sweet wall I'll never see.

And I don't squirt like that genre of squirters:
I gush, an iota deluge, so common and easy
for me that I lie in it after like silk sheeting.

Yet even if I spill this trivia night secret,
there are those who will try to gently or heartily pull up the hoodie
like a delinquent teen, or jam their digits in a hole and I swear
I don't even understand what I'm supposed to feel then. An exam?

I need a deeper pursuit, and if not,
someone to lick at me elsewhere while I milk it,
grind my thighs around that agnostic sponge
or spondee until I'm in a good black hole.
No one will even know. My SATs didn't;
a million math tests endured this way,
at the edge of my plastic seat,
knees together, lips apart,
feet as if at a sewing pedal,
the vague twitch of my hands and jaw
and the whole world none the wiser.

Interapocalyptacourse

The obliteration.

(A convulsing hole.)

How when you fuck me so hard

it hurts, I feel protected.

The end days.

(A blue-hung cliff.)

How when you fuck me so hard

it hurts, I finally relax.

The slipped coil.

(A gaping violence.)

How when you fuck me so hard

it hurts, I believe spring may yet come.

The annihilation.

(A viscous, rhythmic lack.)

How when you fuck me so hard

it hurts, I increase my competencies.

The destruction of the planet.

(A scorched peak.)

How when you fuck me so hard

It's hard to breathe. It's hard
to sleep at night, living in
the crisis world as we come,
through consciousness, to
know it. Is this the postmodern
condition, or was it this way in
1915, 1815? 715 BC? I imagine
it was: every time is a war-time,
an end-time, and we a race of
survival-drivers. Not as good at
it as rats or roaches, but just as
pleasure-hungry, drawn toward
sugar.

The sun will explode. The clean
water will be gone. Nuclear or
meteor, we are not meant to
last. And yet we obsess about
lasting. The only time I don't
obsess about lasting is when
you are graciously destroying
me. That's why I need it harder.
More. *Fuck the pain away,* the
song goes. *Fuck the pain in,*
more like it. The pain is a way
of being alive. An aliveness that
temporarily glosses over, goes
deep, fills a void.

it hurts, I have faith,
or stop caring about faith.

The apocalypse into which
I grind my teeth.
(A swollen weapon.)
How when you fuck me so hard
it hurts, I temporarily imagine
the possibility of safety.

The little death.
(A set of gasps.)
How when you fuck me so hard
it hurts, I drop my burdens
and grow wild and bigger.

The big death.
(A warm abyss.)
How when you fuck me so hard
it hurts, I am the Zen nothing
that connects to everything.

Being in the constant crisis,
one may understandably
want a vaccine. But I've never
trusted Big Pharma, and the
only kind of disruption my
internal systems can bear is
the one that comes from your
well-intentioned slamming of
my internal organs. In these
moments, I think, *I am meant
to be demolished. It is my good
purpose.* In these moments, I
blissfully do not think at all.

Leaf-Peeping

I went by back roads from Maine to Vermont in autumn.

I left my children at home.

I left my husband reading in the room.

I kissed her₁ in her green shirt.

She₁ took off her green shirt and I kissed her there.

She₁ had her children at home, too: like me, she birthed them there and left them there to come meet me.

I let him₂ spank me in front of the other people.

I let him₃ lift up my short skirt to do it, and I bent over.

I let him₄ lift me up and kiss me and I could smell his former life as a smoker.

I put on the Oktoberfest dirndl I bought in college and brought them all beer.

If someone got their own beer, they had to put it back so I could bring it to them.

(In this way too I was made glad.)

I went for a run in the mountains.

I went for a walk in the woods.

I went naked into the hot tub and saw the moon.

Look, I said to him$_5$, the moon.

Where?, he$_5$ said, and arched his head back, showing his clean Viking jaw.

I kissed him$_5$ in the hot tub.

I kissed him$_5$ in the shower with the other people dressing and undressing right outside the stall.

I rubbed my ass against his$_5$ cock in the living room during the dance party, with the rugs rolled back.

I opened my mouth for her$_6$ tongue on the dance floor, with my tongue rolled back.

He$_5$ watched.

(Moon was his$_5$ middle name.)

I dragged a mattress onto the floor by the grand piano.

I lay there waiting for him$_5$.

I lay there crying.

He$_5$ came back and rubbed my arm.

He$_5$ bruised my arm by caring for me so much.

He$_5$ said, Hold still.

He$_5$ said, I said hold still. Don't move until I tell you.

I liked how he$_5$ said it but it was not perfect, not exactly how I wanted it.

I missed my other, and the way he, gently bruises me with the soft warm nap of his, voice: *Baby. Good girl.*

I went for a walk in the fallen leaves and called the other, to tell him, so.

Queers

I drove the country roads
past creatures with their red cataract glint hovering in front of them in
   the bushes
to a red theater to sit with the other queers.

                     I am scratched to flame by testosterone
          and I like the idea of you on T
          and the barrage of what may come with it—
     the up-against-the-wall of it, though that is not always how it goes—

In the red theater:
the girls in their red spangled pasties and black false eyelashes
and the girls in their black ties and black trousers
and M who removed his awkward black slip dress
and awkward black wig to show he'd also removed his breasts
and then knelt on the stage and rubbed the cock he wants so well
there in his black boxer briefs
that my red-lacquered mouth parted
and I leaned forward in my velvet seat.

      When I slip into my red platform maryjanes
I am enacting a gender of my own devising.
A costume that feels more like me than skin.
      I want to feel it. I want it to feel extreme.

I want the physics of ache,
the good pain of having consciously asked for and earned it.

I mean tweak it for me.
Tweak it hard.
I will not default.

Mostly, I am utterly choosing Femme.
I choose it when I take the large steel hedge trimmers
with the red handle and fasten my black and red silk corset
and go out into the yard this sunny afternoon to do the gardening
with a very good posture.
I am examining my Girl. I relish it.
I like how I can feel the steel bones of it for hours after I remove it.

Do you know who I want?
I want you whose hips are the gender
you have been dreaming about forever
like mine become when you cinch me tighter.
I mean I just want you to be thinking about it all the time

your fingers hot and slippery as you lace yourself up into it:
your little black dress;
the big fly flap on the front of your red football pants.

As long as you are into it I'm into it.
As long as I can see how you wear it,
how you wear it so well.
As long as we can breathe into each other's mouths.

I'm sorry it took me all those years of fucking nothing but straight
    vanilla boys
to realize what I most want to fuck is *attitude enacted*.
        I want to fuck you because you've practiced how to walk like that,
how to ditch-drop your voice;
because of the way you constantly mess with your black hair.

        I want to fuck your jump-started, your amped-in, your dragged-
out selfhood.

It's a little red and black velvet theater with the lights out.
Let me go put on my lipstick.

Taproot

I. Issue Four of the magazine has come. It's the Wood issue.

In the pages of contributors' biographies—

Stacy lives in Maine with her husband and two daughters. They raise vegetables and flowers on their organic farm.

Pixie is a writer, sacred space holder and mixed-media artist. Her mentors are wild creatures and her most important teachers are her two strong and feral children.

Brett and her family are sugarmakers. In the time she steals away from the sugarhouse and farmer's market, she moves between garden, daughters and writing.

Jennifer is a full-time artist and mother of two. She recently renovated an old house with her family.

Carrie is a photographer, knitter and designer. She lives in Maine with her husband, daughter and animals, and dreams of living on a small farm someday.

Jenny has a deep interest in home-centric practices.

Julia is a free range journalist, farminista and poet.

Leslie is a writer, gardener, cook and mama. When she isn't writing or changing diapers, she is fermenting, making yogurt, rolling pasta or knitting.

Jessica's family and home keep her inspired as she homeschools, gardens, sews, knits and keeps house.

Ashley, her husband and their young son Huxley, along with a menagerie of chickens, dogs, cats and bees, homestead in North Carolina. Follow her adventures on her blog.

II. Let me state it in an unlovely way.

I kind of hate this magazine and its many beautiful photographs of trees and felt and pumpkins.

I maybe hate it like a twin hates her twin.

I live in Maine. With my husband. With my two children. I knit. I bake. I grow garlic. I write. I change diapers.

This is and is not my life.

This is and is not my aspiration.

I try to escape to it and escape from it.

I am not sure if you love me more or less for it.

I am not sure if I care.

But I will not be writing the pretty poem about homesteading this time, either.

III. My mentor is a wild creature.

On Christmas Eve, as the children hang their felt stockings at their grandmother's house, I flip the phone face up on the coffee table and get the dirty text, so bold it buckles me.

Stop, I text back.

You don't tell me to stop, little girl, he texts.

I call him Daddy. All the time now.

I think about having it inked on an old-school banner on his skin,
surrounded with an anchor and the heart-shaped lock I hope he will
someday use to collar me:
Gets what he wants.

When he gives me the wolf eye, seriouses his mouth and pats his knee, I
hum, and am nothing at all like an actual child, except strong. Except feral.

"Primal Play"

Now you destabilize my sanctum.

Now I clamp my own hand against my mouth because no words.

Now you beg me to let you put it in a little.

Now this is the harder biting.

Now I am wise and uncontrolled.

Now I am triple penetrated.

                              Pin me down. (I am as natural as prey.)

        Feral is a process.

Now I beg you to fill me with creamy biology.

Now I am a grinder.

Now we are the wolf and the dog.

Now we are abandoned and scared of abandon.

Now we are mutated.

Now I prod your yield with two stopped fingers.

                    Be eaten and laid low.

        Feral can be the result of disaster, natural or otherwise.

Now we are not mediated.

Now we are matter.

Now I am a meat.

Now you are not a child, but like a child.

Now I am spread like butter.

Now it is candle-dim and sage.

Push me up against your cave wall.

Feral presents these options for new powers.

I am your fuck animal.

I am nothing, thinkless.

I am obliterated in the soil.

Yes please.

Hops and Barley

Dear reader: I probably shouldn't show you
the most beautiful photograph I have of my face.

It was taken on a day when I was bleeding.

He carefully laid a white towel out over the surface of the hotel bed,
touched my cheek with his fingertips,
then pounded me from behind
until I shouted out and came again and again.
The fucking was an event.
The pleasure was central, enormous, and mine.

Afterward, in the weird liquid light of the marble bathroom,
I looked in the mirror and saw how I'd dissolved.
I felt marathon good, new-tattoo good, birthing good:
triumphant, enduring, burning with adrenalin.
My mouth was swollen and my makeup fuck-smeared into ditches
    below my dilated eyes.
I looked like an iced and slightly crushed slice of cake.
I looked like the victor, my spoils in my teeth.
I looked blurred to calm by bliss.

So I took a photograph of my face with my phone,
and another, and another.

There is nothing in this poem about the country.
This is a poem with a phone that takes photographs in it.
This is hardly a poem at all.

He and I were spending that night in the city.
The view from the concrete balcony of our hotel room
overlooked a cobblestone cul-de-sac and a convenience store,
and beyond that, the fish pier.

The only part of the farm to be found in this poem
is in the thick scent of barley and hops vined in his throat
from what he drank at the German-style hall hours earlier.

And I do love that trace of feathery goldgreen fermentation on him,
the rich rising flora chugging through his blood,
his saliva, his gooey brown eyes.
I love the specifics of it with a wired frenzy, like incantation—
him drinking beer, him drinking beer.
If I were to tell you the true and entire story of our meeting,

you'd know I actually sought him out for this purpose,
found him for this purpose, located him through his lust
for the tight lush buds of these plants
and my lust for his: that what sparks me more than all else
are his indulgent, indolent appetites, encouraged and sated,
including but not limited to icy beverages.
But that is another poem,
one that runs so deep in me I can't quite seem to write it.

Like I can't quite bring myself to show you the photograph
of my mascara pooled under my eyes
after he demolished me facedown into the mattress
until there was nothing left of my psyche
but a raw snake-length of synapse, jumping.

And honestly, I never think I look so pretty
as after I've had him use me this way.

Did You Have a Midlife Crisis on Top of Your Midlife Crisis?
(A Response)

A. I left the city, left my salary, left a daily touching of strangers in other languages on the elevated train and came to this white place with balsam sewn into muslin pouches. Hung the tree swing low.

A. When I tell you about the choice to fuck like I'm now fucking, you ask, *How's Maine?* You worry, maybe, that I'm already bored, that the country is a failure, that the drop-out's a failed experiment, that I have failed in my choices.

That I have, in my own farmhouse, contracted "cabin fever."

A. No, I am not bored. No, I am not sorry.

A. I enjoy watching the bubbles rise in my mason jar of goopy starter. I enjoy spending every day with my dinosaur-obsessed son in my lap while he squeezes the curled tubes of my hair and tells me he is loving me like a predator, with fierceness, which is the biggest quantifier he can imagine. I enjoy knocking the dirt off the purpled bulbs of garlic. I enjoy plainly seeing the harbor zinged with buoys.

A. If sex is a way to be seen, then so are these activities, each a way for me to see myself in the cedar-fenced privacy around my small town home.

A. If being seen is a way to encounter myself and ask a question, then I'm glad I am in my unheated bedroom tonight, next to my husband, reading about rough sex.

A. I never thought I'd want my face slapped as erotic play.

A. I love living in Maine. The air is clean. Most of the children's friends have never watched television. I remember to pick up the onions and fine bright squash delivered from Maia's farm to the backroom of The Green Store. I do not feel lonely. I live in a small town. I don't leave the house some days and still I am not alone. Neighbors walk the block, and at my desk I log in to the black and red screen to comment on the art of begging on a forum about submission. I talk to my girlfriend in Vermont while I fold the laundry, and I talk to my boyfriend in Rhode Island on chat while answering my email.

And sometimes I get in my little blue hybrid car with all the bumper stickers about books and food and love and drive to a hotel or a house in another place, maybe a more urban place, maybe a more rural place, and fuck and love someone to whom I am not legally partnered, while still being married to the man with whom I decided, perhaps foolishly, to let the government have a thing or two to say about our relationship.

A. My husband and I sit down and make the time for all of this, opening our datebooks, which are leather-bound on Mount Desert Island. We talk about what we do while we are doing it and we talk about it after. We don't stop talking about it.

A. This was not the kind of community I thought I was seeking when I came to this life, but it's not *not* the kind of community I was seeking.

A. I would like to put more about the face-slapping into this conversation. I would like to talk to you about it. Or do a demonstration.

A. My desire to have my face slapped on the side of my cheek, where the risk of damage is minimal, immediately after I've cum, uses resources. It takes electricity to book the room at the big hotel. It takes fossil fuels to get the man who will slap me to the lobby of the big hotel. It takes money, which takes time, to pay so that the big hotel will give us a plastic key card for a room. It takes water gushing through the tap of the big hotel to clean up after.

A. But to answer your question: I do not consider this yet an apocalypse, and I am not on lockdown.

A. Some people consider this an apocalypse, and some people are on lockdown, cannot travel, will not travel. Some people cannot, will not fuck for pleasure. Some people cannot, will not love a lot of some people.

A. I find my town a hopeful place. I find it a sheltering field. My sexual pleasure is non-site-specific and mobile, and sometimes happens in the ether, or in text. And before or after my face is slapped to the snap of ecstasy, I want to eat raw honey from Swanville on a spoon and walk to the post office.

A. I can travel. I can fuck. I love a lot of people. I am well, thanks.

Homesteading

Then I thought about you ordering me to get down on my knees like a good girl while I cut back the arugula that was starting to bolt into little white flowers in the raised bed.

Then I thought about over-the-knee boots and short, plaid schoolgirl skirts and ruffle-back panties while scrubbing breakfast off the forks.

Then I thought about my hands on some other girl's round tits while I rode you hard and while right next to me she rode her guy hard while I was pouring boiling water over the mint leaves for tea.

Then I thought about you saying "I'm sorry, baby, but I just have to. Because I want to, and I get to do whatever I want" while I looked up recipes for maple-sweetened almond butter spelt cookies.

Then I thought about you spanking me until I cried and you drying my tears with your thumbs afterward while I pulled the scarlet-white garlic bulbs from the soil and braided the stalks.

Then I thought about you somehow corking all three of my glorious holes at once as I hung the limp clothes on the line to dry in the sun.

Then I thought about my tangled hair wound around your fist while you pounded me as hard as you could as I punched down the sourdough into a neat little ball.

Then I thought about you bathing me all soapy clean in a big tub and burying your tongue in the cleft of my ass while I gently laid the loaf in the floured cloth inside the proofing basket to rise.

Suck

When you lie back with your hands behind your head,
I train you. I tempt and unschool you to be greedy.

No, greedier: I want you selfish as slop.

I want you most when you're sloppy-selfish.

You've always dreamed of this a bit, haven't you?
The 24/7 succubus, the on-my-knees, the wide open mouth?

More, you say, like a baby
(and because I make you say it aloud). *More bj*.

Although your sunning body by a shoreline can set me off,
or you bellied up at a blood-lit dive bar or fluorescent casino buffet,
I prowl for you mostly at night: bat-winged, hooved, fanged.

You want it sucked right out of you,
        all the sorrow, all the marrow,
        long and soft, just as inside the denim as possible.

You want to die.

And in my sweet way, I'll help you.

Stasis

(antonyms: *alteration, modification, revolution*)

A pony in the field,
I am this one's submissive at my prancing best,
broken and proud of it.
I make the decisions.
On all fours, I make things happen.
I am held and can throw.

I am human at first encounter,
and this one is my dominant, shook and bold.
This one wants to be told, wants to be
sold down the river in the little gray boat
of a father's suicide, a mother's cups.
Wants, more than anything now, to be held
like a child, only safe.

Our species likes a stay-the-same life,
and from here rises all samsara, mist in the pasture.
In a seminar, one power-exchange player says,
I think I have a stability fetish,
and everyone in the class laughs softly in recognition.

And yet—the sand bar off the Cape, the old-growth forest—
the dunes, the green canopy, the thin prairie grasses—
the glacier, the mountaintop, the coral reef—
Amy's brown rock wall on the shore,
the clean stream, the desert, by our own devices—

going   going   *gone*

Eat Sleep Fuck

In the winter I am also an animal,   the one who barely rises.

But eats— O! eats.

I am so hungry for you,
     and for salted butter slabbed on a dull, heavy knife,
     and for root vegetables roasted down to caramel,
     and for dark dark chocolate sweetened only with honey.

But mostly for you.

When I am without appetite for work,
     for shampooing the children over their ears,
     for walking out into the fluffed white street,
I am still hungry for you.

When I am flanneled and woodstoved,
     and think I have no hunger for anything
     but deeper unconscious cunting dreams,
     and all my lights are dim to failing,
     February, and I think I have no hunger even for you,
there is still hunger for you.
You lumber up to my driest well and it rushes to spring.

When I have just had you,
      completely full and cozy after
      in the cleft of your flesh,
I am hungry for more.

I rise with my bed hair and I eat sleep (like bear),
but before and after, against your dense underfur,
I lie with you in our dug den and come into myself.

Trinity

If I could go back I would unmarry you,
mark my commitments without government,
in metals and gems and ink,
with the mussel shells above the kitchen sink
and the garlic in the garden

and the new bedchamber for you downstairs
in which I hang the large seascape
so I and the second man can take the upstairs room closer to the
children who sometimes wake at night—

While he and I were away I bought   three etched glass tumblers to
    bring home for us—

Where there was a pair,   now a three-legged householding stool,
                    a structure for which there is no name.

Where there was an apple,   now a pear,   and a berry bush
    budding—

    Come what may—

    I shall scatter my lights—

And if you are not my domestic *only*, my fait accompli?
More and more and more—

Altered Animals

"Fetishism is a translocation of desire . . . The erotic fetish is not merely a symbol of the divine but is itself divine. . . . The fetishist experiences transcendent excitement and complete sensory pleasure; she may experience a nearly religious ecstasy or spiritual melding at the moment of contact with the object; the fetish is a source of aesthetic delight [and] . . . may also be a benevolent force which protects and consoles."
–*Different Loving: The World of Sexual Dominance & Submission*, Gloria G. Brame, William D. Brame and Jon Jacobs

For sure, I breed like a motherfucker, good and true,
but my deep and longest need
lusts nothing to do with sperm or egg,
even prick or cunt or choose-your-
commonly-sexualized part or parcel, north to south.
What I most want, determinedly, is the smell of vice in your mouth
and running down your front, like tonight,
when you had two Scottish ales, one ESB, a pilsner,
and a glass and a half of Sonoma pinot noir
made by the vineyard of a sloppy drunk.

Gosh, I like the hot clocked taste.
Boy, I like the taut swell it makes under your cage
where I stick my sticky fingers between your 4th and 5th
shirt buttons to feel the velvet stretch of your pelt.
When I make contact there, I make contact with the sacred.
With the safe and well.

A tight round belly over a belt reminds me, I think,
of fluid and temporal containments of babies, which I love—
and love reminds me of the sweet indulge,
and you indulging reminds me of you pleasing your whims,
and oh I love that most of all.

Oh and I like the drunk punching through your blood,
the dim slurp in your eyes.
Oh and I like everything full. (Life too.)
Oh and I like how all that ferment
sleepifies you into something sated as an again boy
so that you might conk out and leave me swollen and panting.

To be fucked is a beautiful sacrifice. To be not fucked
is a beautiful sacrifice on the edge of the edge of my thigh.
When you blissful drift off
after I've mapped your perineum and you're done

and I'm not and my empty hole is a nirvana of ache:
I know that this is the sort of thing about which others complain
but the wrong of it undoes me good.
I come from that denial, like some kind of flutter-eyed saint.

Fetish is also the word for a tiny animal
carved to magic its carrier.
Or you can say *paraphilia*, loving what's off to the side.
When you have one, it's oh so specific,
takes place between the 4th and 5th button of your mind.
The devil in the details: the degree of the arch between ball and heel,
the shiny nylon knickers, the last bit of nicotine as it leaves a jaw.
We can't help the appeal.

Maybe jolt-wires collapsing in the brain before birth cause the swerve.
(Some scientists talk about neurons and synapses. Cf. "Hebb's Law.")
All I know is all happy fetishists are somewhat alike:
in an interview, the 'lee from Cleveland says as a child
she jilled off to synonyms for *ticklish* in *Roget's*,
and as a child, I jilled off to synonyms for *gluttony* in *Roget's*.

A tribe of pervs, flushed to this flush since we were kids.
It's in all the cartoons, the black-and-whiter the better:
hamburger eating contests, spanking machines, the girl tied

over and over to the rails in peril.

I got on to Disney's baby elephant hammered on champagne,

Templeton the rat bloated on county fair hot dogs and beer,

vulnerable animals looped, happy

and dopey-dumb, a little out of control.

We too are altered animals.

I like it when you are a bit out of your mind with yum.

I like the evidence of it in and on your flesh.

For whatever reason, deep deep in my magma,

my magnanimous giving over to your pleasure

plunges me into the diamond-mine of mine.

Bang

Some instance of monogamy ends, and the world thinks *over
and done*. Cannot see around the perceived disaster,
limbs everywhere, a vast crater in the scorched earth.

But srsly, folks. What a very long story arc,
that work of undying pairs. What a very long game
of dominoes, of binaries. There *are* other options.

For example, "Monica" went to Central Park
and a Russian on a bike offered her a tour. He was cute,
so she arranged a price and paid it. Off they went; *look at that bush;
look at this tunnel*; he kept turning back to her to call her
beautiful. Put down the bike, she said, because she saw he wanted to,
because she wanted him to. *Hold my hand.*
They walked around the reservoir. They kissed.
She told him about her husband and her seven other lovers.
The Russian said, *I've never met anyone like you.*
If we're going to have sex, "Monica" said,
there are some matters to discuss.
They talked about disease and relationships and,
because she decided they were well-matched in these ways,
she went back to his loft and they showered and he fucked her with his
     enormous cock,

laid her gently in the sheets amidst the condom wrappers,
and returned her to the park by the statue of Alice.

Curiouser and curiouser.
Things like this can happen, in the afterlife which is the here and now.
The post-apocalypse is pink and wild,
edible plants bursting up through the cracks in the cement
and all the water now somehow made potable again
so that when we drink it we—

Mostly you are worried about my children.

But I was fucked to make these children—
they came from fuck, from the way my o
opened and hugged in R's semen in a frothy,
late-summer slick of mucus.

The first baby came from how I wanted a baby
but the second and third came from how I wanted a fuck.
The babies were nice, too,
and I slathered them in my milk
for years on end in bed,
which is another kind of love fluid,
and just as close.
Remember this.

And believe me, I'm a kinder mother
when my bottom is bruised
from the smart round clap of M's open hand.
I'm nicer after.
I'm happier picking up from school
when wearing his high school football jacket and feeling really owned.

I own you, he said that morning, as he held me by the throat
and pushed into me as I squirmed toward and down.
This made me more cheerful

when later I passed out Cheddar Bunnies
and poured raw milk into sippy cups.
When I made dinner while he played with them
the game they love for him to play,
little plastic dinosaurs going on field trips.
Believe me.

Or you know what? Don't.
Just watch them grow.
They are more innocent than most their age,
run laughing screaming naked not-knowing like Eden
around the upstairs rooms each night,
have never heard curse words,
have no shame in their bodies,
talk constantly about love.
What I want for them, now and later,
is their hands on their own pleasure,
their hearts in their own power.
I hope they love as many as they want, with love pouring back.
That they fuck healthfully whom they choose.

That they will be able to say,
We grew up in a warm house
with lots of open-window talking about hard things,

with lots of grown-ups who were loved fully
and loved us truly and we felt safe.
There were pillows and books and a woodstove.
We felt abundance, all ways.
We felt our mother was a full being
who lived thoughtfully, and lived as she pleased.

The Arbor

When I want the deep heat of your more golden skin across my own,
my body makes more glycerol. This is what you call *slippery*.

Mostly, like me, my wetness is water.
But also electrolytes, copper, iron,   and under the low lamp of a
microscope,   you may witness my estrogen-thick fertile cream
drying in a smear on a plate of glass,   the salts crystallizing into the
pattern of a frond.

Testing this response—how when I put my hands on the sweet
convex cathedral   between your pectorals and your belly,
it makes me think of baby names—
                is called *ferning*, or *arborization*.

My slick cervical liquid is as lovely as a tree.
My delight, my pleasure, as lovely as a tree.
        Actually *is* a tree.

Be that as it may, we have tried and tried to find an arbor
under which we can safely and lawfully fuck,
but even in rural Maine, this is hard to come by.

Butch/Bourbon

Mister, I haven't forgotten how, when we worked together back in Chicago, ages ago, before I was a mother, you were the first person who told me about drag kings. And how you took me to my first such show, and how you took me to a burlesque, where, during intermission, your foxy partner and I flashed our breasts at one another as we tried on red sequined pasties across the balcony from where you were seated with your cocktail, and I hoped you were watching.

And I remember the lit-up way I felt when, during the workweek, you and I sat in our little orifices at school and talked about letter-writing and corsetry and our fathers, and you showed me how you had started packing your chinos.

When my oldest was born, we met in a cafe over tea and you gave me her astrological chart as a gift. Later still, raw crystals to sew into silk pillows for dreamwork at the appropriate season. And we discussed food, and farming, and leaving academia to go up to the country, and all along I bit my lip at your bowties, your brogues.

Now I am here in the country and you are still in the city (though now own a lake house) and we are planning a butch/femme tryst at the literary conference out West, a rough-edged shimmering secret in front of everyone we know.

I ask what gender pronoun I should use for you.

Whatever you see.

I ask if I can call you Mister.

You say yes. *And may I call you Kitten?*

Yes. That's what he calls me also. Seems a good sign that you somehow know this.

I text you a picture of myself in garter belt and silken panties, ironing.

You text me a picture of the expensive bourbon you're about to drink.

You don't mind the taste of whiskey breath, do you?

I know only a million ways to say *No, I don't mind.*

Something in the spiked stars, how we've come to this new place.

After, and Before

—After the sex, and the red-velvet swan-sofa'd private clubs with the piles of disposable pads for errant fluids, and the log cabin full of friendly perverts, and the laser light show in the midnight hotel pool, and the couple you grope in the crowd at the Suicide Girls strip show, and the couple you go to barbeque with and talk about your kids, and the sixsome on the tiny short-sheeted twin bed with the math teacher in ponytails, and the swinger websites and feminist porn websites and community-minded fetish websites, then the big What.

—Will I listen to Fresh Air again, and care deeply about pit mining?

—Will there be something on my bedside table other than all this instructive and responsible smut?

—The after comes or doesn't: animal time, the present with no ribbon, no foil, where piss is a warm tribute.

—I live in the house with two maples and a treeswing.

—I did. I do. I will.

—(A speculative conjugation.)

—But really—what arises other than the cleaned-out body?

—Fuck I am spent. In a good way.

—It feels like yellow cake inside me, all done up.

—I mean, I have never had a self *without* desire: since infancy, I have had this same thrumming, more or less. Since infancy, with my cricketish muscles. Since girlhood and my dreams of others' excess. I have always been thick with seed, panting. Inexhaustible. I cannot remember another self.

—The nature of things. Flesh, and the burrowing.

Stroking

It is a pastime,
by which I mean you while your way,
piqued in the flannel bath of sheets
and panting into my grin-open mouth.
Jack it, I beg you. *Jack it.*

You do not need to be asked.
Like a boy: your hand down your shorts,
perennially, snakeroot in bloom.
I love to see you play with your toy.
Sometimes I put my small hand under and we both do yours,
feeling it loosen less and less.

But really my favorite pastime is the stroking of your ego,
to make it as wide and tan
as that massive snake, that warmest root.

I purr into you, red as gold, all my hair up,
and tell you how astonishing your _____, how taut, how divine, how
    edible,
and how I will nurse you through
all the drooping traumas—father's suicide, mother's sodden reaching,
the powder-pink shelter of a former marriage—
and take you someplace where you feel majestic.

Nothing as erotic as expanding you in this way,
glazed over with confidence,
looking at you as a cat may look at a king.

Daddy?
Yes, Kitten?
Jack it for me.

Commons

I have always loved a village green, a commons.
I do not love a commodity,
until I've owned the shit out of it,
and we are twin depleted.

If learning is changing—
if ecology is adaptive and it's we who are stuck in our think-holes—
then fuck me so hard I spot pale pink blood.
Alter me a little.

My body is a commons.
You can pleasure yourself through me
like a haunted house at a theme park.
On the other end, it'll be you all shaky.

I'm not animatronic, a barely clicking swamp.
I'm mowed but still lush, a thoroughfare for glad tidings.

What I am really after is connection.

After We Make a Mess

Don't pass me the frayed bedside cum rag.

I am glad to lie tagged in the viscous graffiti of us all night
until at 2:30 AM I wake scratching through my dream.

Not figuratively—literally:
this stinging brag of an itch
along my smeared valley from from hill to dale,
the yeast (as I imagine it)
in our blended proteins and double-helixes
eating themselves out like tiny fourth of julys
in all my reamed creases and seams.

For at least these hours, let me cease
being such a thinky animal.

Let me stop trying to get clean.

Interlude: I Like Cock

No more poems about the erotic face-slapping?

I think that's enough about face-slapping for now. It doesn't really happen that often.

What about how the guy in California wrote to you through the anonymous website and said, about your man, "His cock looks beautiful inside you"?

I did like that. My man liked it, too. I plan to buy him tube socks with the word HUNG down the side for Valentine's Day.

You talk a lot about size.

Believe me. He walks with it out in front. Cock-led, slightly rolling his gait to accommodate it.

Don't you have anything to say about organic farming?

I wish there was more literature about cock size, the cultural obsession with cock size, specific people's specific obsessions with cock size. Just to get it out in the open, to think about the ways it has caused problems and wars and pesticide use. Theories, articles, chapters, passages about it, like in *The Godfather*, which I haven't read. Cinema, too. Isn't much of literature and cinema really about the patriarchal anxiety over cock size?

Didn't you say you were queer? Starting over? That while you desire The Masculine, that's not about a biological body part?

First of all: ha ha biological body part. There is a biological body part I cannot get over, cannot undo my passion for, and its size is utmost, and it's not a cock.

Second of all, it really is a masculinity thing: I think size queens who fuck male-identified people are as enamored with what a large cock does for a person's ego and confidence and attitude as they are with the cock itself. If a person thinks he has a cock, he has a cock. If a person thinks his cock is huge, his cock is huge.

Third of all, I like cock. As a concept, too.

The Real Thing!

An Invitation to An Encounter

1.

I am indoors, with earbuds, watching media about connecting with nature, and thus the self.

"Where have the simple pleasures of life gone? The beauty of a forest. Just plain breathing."

I am watching on a screen.

2.

It's actually a porn film I'm watching, a "white-coater": the short-lived subgenre of smut in which, to avoid obscenity charges and fall under the "educational" mantle bestowed by the Supreme Court upon *I Am Curious (Yellow)*, the adult industry dressed an actor in a doctor's coat and had him frame the forthcoming X-rated action as a kind of scientific experiment.

But in this Golden Age movie, *Touch Me*, it's not just lip service, and the educator—Dr. Lloyd Davis, we're told, psychologist—is wearing a turtleneck under a blazer as he rearranges the furniture in a Los Angeles suburban home with concrete patio in preparation for the arriving guests.

They're coming for an encounter group, to address the "loss of pleasure" and figure out how to "obtain the highest levels of satisfaction *naturally*, without harm to anyone," Dr. Davis tells us about the marathon session we're about to witness. "Sensual awareness, encounter therapy, sensitivity training"—it goes by many names, its popularity is on the rise, and its "function" is to "try to point out your own inherent potential as a human being."

3.

The human potential movement was and is the term used at Esalen, the Big Sur institute founded by a couple of Stanford grads in the early 1960s, a sacred site for those in search of healing modalities and organic gardens, chanting om by the ocean and building geodesic domes, splashing in naked co-ed hot tubs and joining drum circles.

Think I'm making fun of it? I'm not. Have you been in a naked co-ed hot tub at night with the rain lightly falling down? Have you gone for a walk on the beach at sunrise, eaten mesclun straight from the soil?

Then, like me, you know. They're the real thing, utter delight, connection, some of the best moments of a life. They can make you weep.

4.

I thought of all this a few weeks ago, when the AMC television series *Mad Men* ended its triumphant run.

Along with all the other fans, each locked in our own private box tuned in at 10/9 Central, I watched the final scene: PTSD'd addict antihero straw man Don Draper sitting in lotus position meditating on the grounds of the Institute. There's sun streaming down, and his smoothly spreading smile, and then a cut to the famous, real-life 1971 McCann Erickson television ad known as "Hilltop": fresh-faced, groovy youth belting out "I'd Like to Buy the World a Coke" arm-in-arm. Don's just spent days in encounter groups himself: a gray-haired woman has shoved him, forcefully, silently, into attention, and when he heard another man describe himself as sitting in a dark Frigidaire of existence, Don wept with the man, and held him, and then, perhaps, this epiphany: the multimillion dollar cola jingle heard round the world.

5.

Maybe, like me, you saw this final scene and thought of *Bob & Carol*

& Ted & Alice, perhaps the most famous wife-swapping movie Hollywood's made outside the porn industry, except that no wife-swapping ever actually happens. (We'll get back to that.)

Maybe when you saw Don sitting in the circle, his face a wrench of pain, trapped, his Cadillac long abandoned, you remembered those opening scenes in *Bob & Carol*, the rich hippie couple coasting up the hills in their swooping Jag, landing in a paradise of bare-breasted yogi nymphs and soft-eyed questers groping each other's faces under trees.

Maybe you remember that before all the trippy wallpapered rooms and Dyan Cannon's hair bows waiting for them back in LA, Bob and Carol sat at Esalen for twenty-four hours and pounded pillows with their fists, cried, hugged, said "I love you," and tenderly rubbed the corduroy jeans of a stranger.

6.

Back when it came out, Roger Ebert wrote of *Bob & Carol*: it's a film about "the epidemic of moral earnestness that's sweeping our society right now. For some curious reason, we suddenly seem compelled to tell the truth in our personal relationships." This may be fine for free-wheeling young hippies, Ebert notes, but if adults with careers and spouses and children "start telling the truth too much, they might have to decide who keeps the kids. That's the dilemma."

7.

It's not really Esalen in *Bob & Carol*, just as it's not really Esalen in
Mad Men: neither were permitted to shoot there, the space otherwise
and reverently occupied, then and now, by Herbs for Restoration and
Relaxation, Painting the Outer and Inner Landscape, and The Intention
Masterclass (all offered summer 2015). But it's supposed to be Esalen.
You know it when you see it.

8.

Just because it's a porno doesn't mean it's a send-up. "Don't make a
game of it!" Dr. Davis admonishes when one of the guys gets too handsy
too fast with the girl lying naked next to him. Hard truths are said;
there is sex outdoors. Toward the end of the film, there's role-playing,
which leads to a non-consensual act by Bill, whose partner holds
his head afterward and confronts him about it. Then psychoanalysis
is recommended for this man, since, as the doctor gravely notes,
encounter groups can't get at the kind of hostility Bill holds. The white
coating never disappears: straight through the end, the encounter group
does its work; the doctor stays in his turtleneck and suit; the voiceover
explanation of the encounter techniques plays over the final orgy scenes.

"Your lives won't be changed," the good doctor says as they all depart, "Don't expect too much from a forty-eight hour encounter! But I do think you're all freer in your feelings than when you arrived. Good luck to all of us."

"Bill," he continues, "Promise to call me Monday: I want to give you the name of that psychologist." Can a blue movie be educational, be *for real*? Can a tv show about advertising? Can a late 60s social comedy?

9.

Bioethicist Jonathan Moreno has been studying the legacy of his father, J. L. Moreno, a psychiatrist who published "Invitation to an Encounter" in 1914, a design for a radical style of group therapy that involved techniques borrowed from experimental theater, and his own innovation, psychodrama, which entailed role-playing and other now-standard practices.

From these first experiments came T-groups, aimed at mid-century shell-shocked vets (like Don Draper), and then other kinds of group therapies for people with some issues (but not serious mental illness) to work through This was a new use for therapy: to unlock "human potential." There were sensitivity training groups for corporations, and the Esalen-style encounter groups and the consciousness-raising groups of the 1960s and 70s, and the many kinds of group therapies that permeate our culture today.

It all goes back to performance.

10.

Just as Dr. Davis says in *Touch Me*, the couple in *Bob & Carol* tell their straight-laced friends Ted and Alice afterwards at a fancy restaurant "no one was miraculously cured" at Esalen.

"It doesn't work that way. But just saying something out loud, in front of a room of strangers, is the beginning of something."

11.

I am a person who likes intention, who likes to say things aloud in a room of strangers, who likes to look things in the face. Who craves *authentic encounters*.

It's what I want when I look at art, when I lace up my hiking boots, when I give birth to a baby, when I stand at the front of a classroom, when I press my body up against others in front of the stage at a concert, when I fuck.

I think I've always been this person.

I think it's why I cried when I watched *Woodstock* on video as a teenager: stood up from the beige couch in the den and wept, openly, at the mud and the face paint and the tai chi in the grass, all things I was missing in my split-level ranch in the mid-1980s.

I have never stopped weeping like this. I still want these authentic experiences out in the counterculture the way some want meat, or water. And I'll take it on film if I must, if it's been a bit too long since my own feet were bare at some summer rock festival, or since I was on a bed full of naked bodies intertwining like ivy on a vine.

12.

"We're trying to *deal* with things," Bob and Carol say. "We're trying to stop playing games with the people we love." ("Don't make a game of it," says Dr. Davis.)

"Beautiful," Bob and Carol say, about everything, including an admission of an affair, an insult, anything honest. "The truth is always beautiful."

13.

This is meant, maybe, as satire, these people in their velvet jackets and Hermès scarves constantly saying "beautiful."

But they have a sense of humor about it: "so groovy and peaceful," Carol says of herself, carrying the canapé tray after a dinner party. They're not in a cult. They are good, loving parents to their happy child: errant trike in the Spanish-tiled hallway, Bob giving piggybacks before bedtime.

They are smart, and successful, and happy.

14.

And you know what? I buy it completely. Perhaps you will think me cheesy, or naïve. Perhaps this means I *am* cheesy, or naïve. That I'm New Age. I do own a few tarot decks. I do light a balsam-scented candle every now and then.

And, don't tell, but like Bob and Carol, I've sat on a bed next to the person my partner just fucked and had a far-out, honest conversation. Like Carol, I have not felt jealous (though thought at first, as she does, "Maybe I'm kidding myself.")

I've sat under trees and felt the faces of strangers with my fingertips, stood naked opposite a man I didn't know—almost bald, hard of hearing, wrinkled—and looked into his eyes and felt my heart swell. And it was beautiful.

15.

After the finale of *Mad Men*, the viewing public is divided: has Don reached nirvana, or has his spiritual quest resulted in a successful ad campaign? Is it meant to be cynical? Or a coincidence? Has he "found" anything at all? What's the meaning of all this?

16.

The day after the last episode of the show, I go to pick up the kids from school with my hair in two braids with ribbons on them, like the receptionist at Don's retreat, like the girl in the real Coke ad. My friend Robin, a fellow film geek waiting for his own son there in the cafeteria, immediately spots the sartorial reference and starts humming, "I'd like to teach the world to sing."

We talk about the last scene of *Mad Men*, and about the last scene of *Bob & Carol*. "What the world needs now," he sings. "It's so creepy!" He's talking about the Vegas casino eye-gazing, the "Hilltop"-like parade of groovy nations, the actors staring directly and lovingly into the camera: authentic connection right there on the Strip. "It's not creepy!" I say, pouting a bit in my retro braids.

How to convince him? How to convince you, without taking you to Esalen and keeping you there long enough that you, like Don, have a breakthrough, land at some insight, or at least join hands with me?

17.

Maybe my religious-slash-spiritual practice is encounter groups. Or non-monogamy. Not what comes from these, but the activities themselves: the moment of touching the face of the new and possibly previously-unattractive-to-me person and knowing I can love them, that I do love them.

18.

How did encounter groups get conflated with swinging anyway? The low-fi indie film *Computer Chess* is set at a dumpy hotel overrun with cats, where programming geeks holding a small convention collide with an even smaller bunch of people there to take part in an encounter group. When one of the computer guys wanders into the wrong conference room, the encounter group sits on the floor and rebirths him through their arms to set him free. It doesn't work, nor does the invitation for a threesome with a well-meaning, middle-aged, nurturing couple who want to release an MIT grad student from his virginal repression.

Watching this movie, I thought the couple—sane-seeming, friendly, the wife a bosomy blond with a sweetly maternal air—were convincing swingers, neither repulsive nor "Ken and Barbie," as the common parlance in the lifestyle goes. But a piece in *Cinema-Scope* by Phil Coldiron calls them "the last sad remnants of the American '60s via a group of free love proponents," and the review in *Film Comment* calls the encounter group "hilarious."

I think the encounter group seems interesting and is after something useful and important, and the swinger couple is cute and sexy and make the young nerd a good offer in good faith. Does this say more about me than the film?

19.

"Insight!" Carol and Bob take to uttering, wide-eyed, as they come to some next paradigm shift. "Lights going on in my head!"

I know it's supposed to be a joke, or that, at least, it's received by the audience largely as joke.

That even back then the whole thing seemed kooky, implausible, stupid.

And by 2015 we are supposed to mostly notice how dated it all is: the outta sight convertibles and suede miniskirts as wacky as the ideas about self-expression and world peace.

And listen, I do want to buy exactly Natalie Wood's baby-doll nightie.

But when Robin says *creepy* of the final scene in *Bob & Carol* as if it were the marble-eyed ending of *The Stepford Wives,* I want to cry. Because I cry *with* that scene. I believe in it.

And if the orgy before Tony Bennett never happens? Well—it's pretty advanced non-monogamy to fuck your best friends and have it all work out fine. I know lots of couples who've been through that: it's tricky to pull off. It's Swinging PhD. But can you get under the covers with some nice people with whom you have drinks, and have them then show up for your kid's birthday party at the pool, and live to tell? Absolutely. Trust me on this.

I can tell you more later, if you're interested. If you're open to it.

20.

Maybe all of this ought to be parodied, and I should be seen as ridiculous myself, and the number of times I say *authentic* should become a drinking game. But what else is there?

Tell me a better use of one's time than trying to find the real thing.

Bob & Carol & Ted & Alice (1969), dir. Paul Mazursky

Woodstock (1970), dir. Michael Wadleigh

Touch Me (1971), dir. Anthony Spinelli

Computer Chess (2013), dir. Andrew Bujalski

"Person to Person," *Mad Men* (S7, Ep14, 2015), dir. Matthew Weiner

Things That'll Chew You

"We're here to devour each other," my son says.

I thank him for this, and kiss him goodbye, so I can go off with my boyfriend, the one my son calls "the gorilla," to a clothing-optional spiritually-driven sex camp in the rolling hills of riverside Maryland for a few days of pagan-inspired springtime romping.

*

There are ritual temples and a full-moon orgy by a bonfire with live drumming and sacred whore goddess work and polyamorous processing and pole dancing and people on leashes and people in kilts and people in corsets and people with flowers in their hair and glitter on their cheeks. There is attention paid to pronoun usage and tantric encounter groups where we sing our secret names to one another and weep. There is plenty of fucking in the grass.

I buy a dress that looks like butterfly wings from a woman in a leather loincloth.

*

But in the class on the topic of "energy" we attend in a rustic cabin, I don't like the instructor, who is staying in our bunk, and has seemed flighty and desperate, with a sullen partner who checks his cell phone in bed. When we're given a guided meditation and told to enter the room of our consciousness through the glowing indigo orb of our third eye, I picture a black void, boundaryless.

"Now decorate it," the teacher says.

I will not, I think. My void needs no décor.

"Now find a safe space to lie down in it."

I do not want a safe space. I dissolve myself.

"Now look out a window to your daily life."

My void has no window. I know I am being petulant, which is not perhaps the most evolved of states, but I don't care: I didn't make a window earlier, and won't go back and bang one out now.

"Now know that you can decorate your daily life in the same way you decorated your room."

I grab my boyfriend by the hand and we dash out of the cabin, exhaling only once we are ten yards away.

*

On our way home from sex camp, there's a TGIFridays in every town along I-95 from Maryland to Massachusetts.

I wave my hands and now they, too, are a gorgeous void.

*

I hope I will meet a wild animal in the road, and that it will be the death of me.

Dreamy

In spite of all I've said about your heft and sirloin,
the truth is you are sometimes a scared boy.

Let's be honest: you are mostly (also) a scared boy.

And so when in the seam of the night
I awake to find us as always interlaced and facing
but this time you muttering tiny trembling words
under your heavy porn star mustache,
sibilant whispered chatter,
I strain to translate and can only discern your fear.

I stay still with you until the rush of smudged protest abates,
then very slowly touch your right thigh with my left hand,
short strokes, to comfort you.
And you swell against me then and pulse, thrusting slightly,
like you do, like a dog.
I stroke; you swell, pulse, thrust.
I do this till you stir
and I flip to push my plush bottom against what is now solid,
as I do, homing.
You sigh in relief and graze one hand from my neck to my knee.

Do you remember your dream?

Not really, you say, pulling me closer. And then: *O yes. I was fucking someone.*

Yeah you were.

You laugh and sink inside me, flash art. *How could you tell?*
You were talking but I couldn't make it out.
You seemed afraid, so I touched you, and you got hard and started bucking.

From deep inside me you say sleepily, *I was being interrogated by one after another. I was in trouble.*
And then I realized the last person to question me was someone I could seduce.
And that person and I were fucking.
You changed the course of my dream.

A man's dream.

I begin to fall back to sleep as you push your way through me,
the slop of it audible from under the dark brown blanket,
and half into my own dream I think,
Stroking you is a temporary hold on the mail.

Desire, perhaps from the Latin, meaning "from the Stars"

If this were a performance piece,
and I were here in my guise as clairvoyant or derby girl or park ranger,
I would start with you on the inside of my body, crawling outward.

I would lift my skirt.

I would have a skirt.

I would have a skirt made of newsprint,   a skirt made of
    mustache, a skirt made of bourbon,
        a skirt made of "vexed feminine heteronormative desire."

In the performance piece of this poem,
I would sing the date-rape-drug lyrics from "Blurred Lines,"
        and in so doing, would queer the lens and be the good girl who
    actually does want it.
I would turn my backside to you and show you how,   as a white girl,
I'm succeeding in my utter failure to twerk.

In the performance version,   you would be the audience as
    consensually DP'ed.

There would be a carefully pre-negotiated cathartic gang bang
in the middle,   right here,   and then aftercare.

We would all be dressed like animals, with animal masks.
This means we would all be undressed and happy
and sniffing each other without antiperspirant.
No one in the bookstore or theater
would be wearing talc or aluminum.
This means we'd all be "skyclad," which would mean that in the
performance piece,   we'd drink from the same glass of
passed wine   and burn our regrets in a straw effigy.

I want to do the performance of this poem
in which I lie down in the middle of this room.
In which, to form a middle, we form a circle of people.

No, in the real version, we'd be in the middle of a clearing.
        The middle of a meadow.
        The middle of a stamen.
        I'd project at you from the middle of pollen.

Then I'd pause here and masturbate to orgasm   using only interior
muscles you can't see   unless,

again,   you were listening from within my body,   which you could be:
I can hold up to sixty-five listeners on the inside of my body for this piece.

I could bring down the stars.

Re-pleat

last night the little one sat up in his bed&pajamas,
puked yellow over all five stuffies, the wall
& the Cerberus parents had to strip all the bedding in the dark

& I put Vaseline under the bigger one's chafed nostrils all day

& my eyes are onions, with a decorative lump under the right

    (in case you were thinking, dear reader, as D did, that this
    polyphonic is a constant spree, *replete with comforts*

& this morning the bear-man & I
twin-star dreamed of his libido & woke enwrapt

so I moved down the wine-pouch of his body
& swallowed without spilling

    this too

    this very plain&happy poem w/ its bodily fluids

    this plaiting, this pleating

I Do Not Want to Fuck You Captain America

The difference between you and me, Fanboy, (and perhaps between the Masculine and the Feminine if you want to talk about it that way) is that I don't have a single tiny need for any flying ships with glowing moonstone eyes that could swallow an ocean. I don't want any blue flashing gadget cream screens with secret codes for my birthday, or flashing laser face screens or tongue recognition software. (I want to flash my tongue on the soft landscape.) I have no craving for a jet big as a blinking planet. I have no lust for wheels that retract or blades that boomerang back to a holster or zapping metal arms that can take down a barricade or headphones that collapse into a small bronze bullet case. I don't want a heavy shield with a circled star: I am not so afraid, really, to die.

What scares me: anti-depressant run-off in the creek; estrogen pill run-off in the pond. A lack of nuance in stories; a surplus of lazy thinking in the media. Someone undermining, on purpose, my child's confidence. This life of machines, where you and I aren't given enough hours to be animals together.

Seriously. I don't want a many-bridged matrix structure of brushed steel with wall-sized electronic maps of global villainry and loaded shaft guns and swaths of plate glass perpetually shattering and encrypted light-up thumb drives and little red digital target marks on absolutely everything. With the terrible destruction vehicle bursting through the side of the office tower. (A comic book nightmare that came true, remember? Ash and shards and falling bodies, a city smoking in the distance, just like in the movie. This was not a movie.)

This is not a movie, and when I think about you fucking me, I am not thinking of the Millennium Falcon. I am not thinking, This government protects us from vulnerability and surveillance, and this government surveys us, and this government made us vulnerable in this way. I am not thinking, How can I stay safe? When we are fucking, I am not trying to protect myself. In fact, I am trying to not protect myself.

I do not want you juiced with serum so you can save the world. I do not want you juiced at all.

Fanboy, lie down and crawl back into your fur. Give up your need for toys. Be a bear cub again.

How I Have Evolved

"In the 5 million years since early hominids first emerged from east Africa's Rift Valley, the Earth's climate has grown increasingly erratic. Over cycles lasting hundreds of thousands of years, arid regions of central Africa were overrun by forests, forests gave way to grasslands and contiguous landscapes were fractured by deep lakes. It was within the context of this swiftly changing landscape that humans evolved their sizable brains and capacity for adaptive behavior, said Rick Potts, director of the Human Origins Program at the Smithsonian Institution National Museum of Natural History. In such a world, the ability to think creatively . . . proved to be a major asset, he said."
—"Humans May Be the Most Adaptive Species," Nathanael Massey, *Scientific American*, Sept. 25, 2013

I now only go to the academic panels about "queerness," "eros" or
    "nature".
I now only go to panels where the scholar sings from the podium.

I've learned that what I like best about The Daddy
is the cuff links, the takedown, the scotch neat,
and the layer of delicious fat that suffocates me when I'm on bottom.

Despite the semantic disjunction,
I recognize that the phrase in common usage is *blow-bang*, not *gang-blow*.

I know how to say *Your bruises look beautiful,*
admire the trail of angel-wing blood on your back from the removed
    needles.

I love, like a gay man, the kinds of other men who, when they pass,
cause one to say *WOOF.*
I want to buy a t-shirt that says *WOOF.*

I am aware of the splendor of humiliation.

I know I am more subversive in the space
when I do not shave my head, ink up, pierce or trucker cap,
when I aim my breasts nearly just completely out of my little black dress.

You can talk to me about International Mister Leather and I am with you.

I believe that failing is another kind of win.
But that the wrestling is the sweet part, the process.

The Grid

I will tell you the dirtiest secret: all this "play"

is just   a way to make the bright red strings
of invisible power

      that matrix through our everyday doings
      visible.

    Like the tiny silver padlock I wear on a chain around my neck

  to tell the world I am owned

which the world does not understand

    which is what I like about it:

the hush

    of the joining mechanism.

Every magic hour
    I am engaged

in some   reification   destruction   subversion
acclimation   implication

of power gone awry.

       And not just the grid.

I am a worker.

       A parent.   A broker.   A boss.

Property.
           Owner.

I have a mortgage two children two dogs this checkbook with vinyl cover.

I owe money to the electrician.

All of this could be a devastatement

an anxiety attack   a reason for more Advil   more Ativan

and thus a cause of more run-off   more
downstream

and thus a cause for cancer.

Or all of this could be an erotics   should I so choose.

And I so choose.

My deep gratitude to the editors and journals who took (to) these poems:

ADULT, American Poetry Review, Ampersand, Animal, Bedfellows, Black Clock, BOMB, Boston Review, Bright Wall / Dark Room, Dusie, Interim, Little Star, OCHO, PEN American, Secret Behavior, Tin House, Tinderbox, Volta, Washington Square

I feel enormously fortunate that this book is a Four Way Book, and that Sally Ball was my deep-thinking, open-hearted, meticulous editor. This project is much stronger for her guidance and this home.

Heartfelt thanks to the writers, friends and listeners—including a lot of wonderful sex-positive feminist and queer writers whose work has inspired me—who were open to these poems and the surrounding conversations. I am thinking right now of Carley Moore, Sarah Vap, TC Tolbert, Sinclair Sexsmith, Tina Horn, Kristin Sanders, Elizabeth Hall, Khadijah Queen, Wendy C. Ortiz, Andrea Lawlor, Roan Boucher, Stephanie Berger (aka "The Madame"), Madison Young, Carina Finn, Janet Hardy, Siouxsie Q James, Laura Seaton, Kim Brooks, Marybeth Sweeney, Tristan Taormino and the OG "Girl Gang"—Ally Bebbling, Joslyn Kite and B Van Hoene—and other Gang-affiliated students including Laura Winberry, Caitlin Vestal, Shannon Harwood, Brigitte Lewis, Sally Hollister and Shareen Murayama. Enormous gratitude to Rob Bywater, who took this journey with me. And, most of all, to Mikey Simone, who altered the course of my history and continues to do so every day. Happily, there are many others to thank as well. I love you and the ways you live and the things you make.

Arielle Greenberg's previous poetry collections are *Come Along with Me to the Pasture Now, Slice, My Kafka Century,* and *Given.* She's also the writer of the creative nonfiction book *Locally Made Panties,* the transgenre chapbooks *Shake Her* and *Fa(r)ther Down,* and co-author, with Rachel Zucker, of *Home/Birth: A Poemic.* She has co-edited three anthologies, including *Gurlesque,* forthcoming in an expanded digital edition co-edited with Becca Klaver. Arielle's poems and essays have been featured in *Best American Poetry, Labor Day: True Birth Stories by Today's Best Women Writers,* and *The Racial Imaginary,* among other anthologies. She wrote a column on contemporary poetics for the *American Poetry Review* and edited a series of essays called *(K)ink: Writing While Deviant* for The Rumpus. A former tenured professor in poetry at Columbia College Chicago, she lives with her family in Maine, where she writes, edits, teaches, and works for a creative services agency.

Publication of this book was made possible by grants and donations. We are also grateful to those individuals who participated in our 2019 Build a Book Program. They are:

Anonymous (14), Sally Ball, Vincent Bell, Jan Bender-Zanoni, Laurel Blossom, Adam Bohannon, Lee Briccetti, Jane Martha Brox, Anthony Cappo, Carla & Steven Carlson, Andrea Cohen, Janet S. Crossen, Marjorie Deninger, Patrick Donnelly, Charles Douthat, Morgan Driscoll, Lynn Emanuel, Blas Falconer, Monica Ferrell, Joan Fishbein, Jennifer Franklin, Sarah Freligh, Helen Fremont & Donna Thagard, Ryan George, Panio Gianopoulos, Lauri Grossman, Julia Guez, Naomi Guttman & Jonathan Mead, Steven Haas, Bill & Cam Hardy, Lori Hauser, Bill Holgate, Deming Holleran, Piotr Holysz, Nathaniel Hutner, Elizabeth Jackson, Rebecca Kaiser Gibson, Dorothy Tapper Goldman, Voki Kalfayan, David Lee, Howard Levy, Owen Lewis, Jennifer Litt, Sara London & Dean Albarelli, David Long, Ralph & Mary Ann Lowen, Jacquelyn Malone, Fred Marchant, Donna Masini, Louise Mathias, Catherine McArthur, Nathan McClain, Richard McCormick, Kamilah Aisha Moon, James Moore, Beth Morris, John Murillo & Nicole Sealey, Kimberly Nunes, Rebecca Okrent, Jill Pearlman, Marcia & Chris Pelletiere, Maya Pindyck, Megan Pinto, Barbara Preminger, Kevin Prufer, Martha Rhodes, Paula Rhodes, Silvia Rosales, Linda Safyan, Peter & Jill Schireson, Jason Schneiderman, Roni & Richard Schotter, Jane Scovell, Andrew Seligsohn & Martina Anderson, Soraya Shalforoosh, Julie A. Sheehan, James Snyder & Krista Fragos, Alice St. Claire-Long, Megan Staffel, Marjorie & Lew Tesser, Boris Thomas, Pauline Uchmanowicz, Connie Voisine, Martha Webster & Robert Fuentes, Calvin Wei, Bill Wenthe, Allison Benis White, Michelle Whittaker, Rachel Wolff, and Anton Yakovlev.